THAMYRIS

TO-DAY AND TO-MORROW SERIES

E. P.   D U T T O N   &   C O M P A N Y

THAMYRIS

OR

Is there a Future for Poetry?

BY

R. C. TREVELYAN

NEW YORK
E. P. DUTTON & COMPANY
681 FIFTH AVENUE

808
T7

PN
1031
T7
1925a

To

The Memory of

OSWALD SICKERT

CONTENTS

THAMYRIS

THAMYRIS

CHAPTER I

THE MUSES IN HEAVEN

THERE is an old Teutonic legend that every year, upon All Souls' Day, the archangel Raphael is sent down to the classical ward of Hell, where the dispossessed deities of heathendom are confined, with a summons for the nine Muses to appear and give a command performance before the throne of Jehovah and the assembled Host of Heaven. So the poor embarrassed ladies, ushered before that critical and unsympathetic audience, reluctantly tune their lyres, and begin some ancient Hellenic chant, some ode, it may be, that they had once sung in the feasting-hall of Olympus, or at the marriage of Cadmus and Harmonia. At first their strange pagan minstrelsy seems harsh and unpleasing to blessed ears, accustomed only to the angelical modes of " saintly shout and solemn jubilee "; but before long, in spite of themselves, the angels are touched and troubled by this disquieting music, burdened with all the passions and sighs of humanity, until at last celestial visages are stained with tears, and the sound of weeping is heard in Heaven.

But on one of these occasions, not so very long ago, after the Muses had come to the end of their program, several of the more literary archangels expressed a desire to hear some examples of post-classical poetry, of which they knew little or nothing. As the Muses

THE MUSES IN HEAVEN

could not gratify their curiosity, Satan, who, as in the *Book of Job,* was paying one of his rare visits to the court of Jehovah, stepped into the breach, and beguiled several hours with poetical specimens from different periods, which he had picked up during his ceaseless wanderings to and fro upon the earth. At first his audience was enchanted. He had an excellent ear and memory, and could reproduce perfectly the several styles of the troubadours and minnesingers, and of the various courtly or popular minstrels of the Middle Ages. But gradually a change came over his performance. The saints and angels grew puzzled and restless, as the element of song, and even of intonation, progressively disappeared, until at last they found themselves listening with pain and indignation to mere naked, spoken verse. And what verse? Rime they were familiar with in their hymns, and liked. But soon even rime began to fade, and threatened to vanish altogether. Metre too dissolved and degenerated from all regular recognisable form; and when finally Satan jerked out the latest jewel of American *vers libre,* he was greeted, as once before in Hell, with a dismal universal hiss, the sign of public scorn. The Muses had long ago fled down horror-stricken to Hades; and Satan, who always dislikes unpopularity, smiled, bowed, and retired. The choirmaster, Gabriel, tapped the desk with his baton, and a moment later the Heavenly Host was purging its offended ears with the strains of a noble Gregorian chant.

Now what lesson, if any, may we draw from this apologue? Were the angels right, or wrong, or perhaps neither? Has the history of poetry been merely a deplorable tale of decadence, a progressive impoverishment and deterioration, through senility and second-childishness, towards an unlamented death in a bastard and graceless prose? Or on the contrary has the gradual divorce of poetry from music and intoning meant its liberation for subtler and more rational, but no less truly poetic purposes? Before attempting to answer such questions, let us first look at the historical facts.

Homer, the fountain-head of Hellenic, and so of European poetry, though originally sung to the accompaniment of a lyre, was in later times intoned by professional rhapsodists, much as most Oriental poetry is intoned to this day. Greek lyrical poetry was of course always sung, whether chorally or by soloists. The dialogue of Greek plays was not sung, but was probably intoned, or at least declaimed in a highly conventional and rhythmical manner, which was perhaps not so very unlike the still-surviving tradition of the Japanese Nō play-actors. It is uncertain whether Horace intended his *Odes* to be read, or to be sung to the lyre: but Lucretius and Virgil un-

doubtedly wrote their poems to be read.
Virgil indeed gave public readings of
his *Eclogues*. Probably, could we hear
gramophone records of his perform-
ances, we should say that he was intoning rather than reading. However that may be, his example set a
fashion that was disastrous for Latin
poetry. His successors wrote more
and more with a view to declamation,
not in the noble Homeric manner, but
in a style that was both bombastic
and amateurish; and so poetry soon
degenerated into stale rhetoric and
boredom.

When after the lapse of centuries
poetry emerged again, rejuvenated, its
infant energies were still schooled by
the same two mistresses, music and
intonation. The art of the rhapsodists
of the *Chanson de gestes* may have been
ruder than that of the Homeridae, but
its æsthetic character and its social
function were much the same. And for
centuries the medieval lyric was in-

tended to be sung, not read. But with
the multiplication of books the inevitable change began to operate, and the
medium of poetry came more and more
to be verse spoken and read, rather
than performed.

The poetical drama of the sixteenth
and seventeenth centuries was, from
a historical point of view, no more than
a brief and glorious episode. The
declamation of dramatic verse may well
have been a great art on the English,
French and Spanish stage; but, if so,
it has not survived into our own time,
and shows little sign of resurrection.
The development of polyphonic and
instrumental music, while it has made
modern opera and the *Lieder* of
Schubert and Brahms possible, seems
to have destroyed all hope of an equal
marriage between music and lyrical
poetry. Modern polyphony is a great
art, but a tyrannous; and though a
beautiful poem may still inspire a
beautiful setting, the medium of the

resulting work of art will be musical,
and not poetic. Verse no doubt can
still be declaimed, whether on the stage
or elsewhere; but actors have generally
neither taste nor tradition; the poets
themselves have seldom enough skill or
training to be effective; and professional reciters are " abominable, un-
utterable, and worse." Thus it would
seem that all the avenues which might
lead to the public performance of
poetry are blocked. There are either
no roads at all, or those that exist are
in the possession of road-hogs. Is this
state of things a distaster or no? And
if it be a disaster, are there any remedies
to be found?

It is no doubt possible that so
summary a diagnosis may be quite
misleading. Chaucer, it might be
objected, already wrote for readers;
and so did Milton. Yet many of us find
them, and some of their successors, still
quite readable. Surely then great
poetry can still be both produced and

enjoyed, even when it is completely divorced from music or intonation. All this may be true. Yet it is well to remember that Chaucer was the immediate successor on the one hand of the English and French minstrels, and on the other of Dante and Boccaccio, whose art in its turn grew directly out of that of the troubadours and the Italian minstrels. And who have been the inheritors of Chaucer's art? Spenser, let us say, and in our time William Morris. Is it not possible that both Chaucer and Dante were peculiarly fortunate, in that their art had only quite recently emerged from the discipline of a more primitive musical stage? Their successors may be said to have deteriorated, the more purely literary they became, and the further removed from the Pierian fountain-head of minstrelsy. Then again Milton, though more than any other English poet he was consciously the heir to all the ages, inherited his medium

and his metrical technique directly
from Shakespeare's verse that was
written, not for reading, but for
dramatic performance, although no
doubt Milton modified it considerably
for his own undramatic purposes. As
to the inheritors of Milton's art, such
as Wordsworth and Keats, Matthew
Arnold and Mr. Bridges, considerable
as have been their achievements, are
there not some signs, even in their own
work, and still more in the tendency of
recent experiments, of an impulse to
break away from Miltonic and Shakespearian usage, as though the medium of
blank verse could no longer be profitably
explored, not at least in its old traditional form?

Nevertheless it might plausibly be
maintained that although the poets of
the future are not likely to repeat the
particular successes of Chaucer and
Milton and their school, there is no
reason why they should not exploit the
medium of spoken verse in quite new

ways, just as successfully as did their predecessors. First however it would be as well to become somewhat clearer as to the nature of this medium of spoken and silently read verse, and how it differs from more primitive poetry.

CHAPTER II

THE MEDIUM OF SPOKEN VERSE

WHEN we read Homer or Aeschylus to ourselves, we do not as a rule attempt to imagine what their poems must have sounded like, when they were recited or sung. We transpose them, as it were, into a medium more or less resembling that of modern poetry. Let us try to measure what our loss must be, and what, if any, the compensations. To begin with, the elements of music and intonation, and also, in drama, of acting and dancing, have disappeared altogether. The intensity and mass of our emotions cannot possibly be the same as they would have been, could we have heard and beheld the living reality of which the text is but a pale, colourless shadow. It is true that rhythm is still there, and the general proportions of the whole: but rhythm and movement, unembodied and uninterpreted by performers, are far more difficult for us to realise by the less sensuous, more purely mental process of reading; while in the absence of musical and histrionic contrasts and emphasis, even the general proportions are likely to be somewhat obscured. It is as though we were studying a photograph or a monochrome copy of a painted picture; or rather we might be said to experience the same kind of difficulties as when we are contemplating colourless fragments of Greek sculpture against the background of a museum wall, at a distance and in a light that were never intended for them by their creators. How different would be our emotions, could we see the figures of the Olympian or Parthenon pediments placed in their right relation to the architecture and to the landscape, unmutilated, and glowing with colour which harmonised with that of the temples of which they were an organic part! It is a poor compensation that by long loving study we may perhaps become more intimate with the indestructible beauty of certain details, than we could ever have been, had we seen them less closely as elements of a complex work of art.

In some ways our plight with regard to ancient poetry is less unhappy. Many of our texts are unmutilated, and when we read the *Oedipus* to ourselves, it should seem to us as much an organic unity as *Othello*. There may also be a real gain in our sensitiveness to the more purely literary qualities, such as verbal, as distinguished from musical colour, the suggestive values of words and combinations of words, their overtones, and the complicated reverberations they evoke in our minds. As none of the work is being done for us by performers, our imagination, thrown back on its own unaided resources, should be all the more wide awake and active. A line drawing is often a more effective stimulus to the mind than a painting, an unaccompanied violin sonata than an orchestral symphony; and in the same way poetry, when merely read to ourselves, though it cannot so imperiously dominate our physical senses, may well make a subtler and profounder appeal to the intellectual imagination.

All that has been said with regard to the reading of poetry that was intended to be sung or chanted, should be even more true of modern verse that has been written solely in order to be spoken or read. Such poetry is in fact composed in quite a different medium to the poetry of Homer and Aeschylus; and I must now try to make it clear what this medium seems to me to consist of. In order to do so, I must venture upon a brief excursion over the perilous quicksands of metrical theory. To save time I shall speak dogmatically, while well aware that none of my assertions can at best do more than express a part of the truth.

When we read aloud a leading article, or any other piece of utilitarian and unemotional prose, we are not as a rule in the least aware of the rhythm of the sentences. But suppose we were to read the same leading article with a simulated mock-heroic emotion, we should then find, if we cared to observe, that we were now emphasising the before latent rhythm in two ways: we should be stressing certain syllables with greater force; and at the same time we should be making the intervals between these stressed syllables, not indeed rigidly equal, but far more nearly equal than they were, when we read the passage with the lack of emotion which it merited. And we shall find that the same thing happens whenever we read prose that genuinely moves us. Emotion in fact always tends to regularise and emphasise rhythm, even in prose. Now the main function of verse is deliberately, by its structure, to regularise rhythm, and so to create emotion artificially. Let us take a normal English verse: "The curfew tolls the knell of parting day." The five stressed syllables, *cur- tolls, knell, par-, day,* are felt to be equi-distant in time. No doubt they are in fact only approximately equi-distant. The human voice is not an instrument like a piano or a violin, by means of which we can divide time into mathe-matically equal spaces. However, the normal bars, or feet, are *felt* to be equal in time; and that is sufficient. The rhythmically indeterminate words and phrases of everyday speech are forced into this mould, or rather stretched upon this framework; and that process is a continuous series of Procrustean operations, of slight lengthenings or contractions, and imperceptible changes of stress and emphasis. Almost the most important difference between good and bad verse is that in good verse this process of moulding and stretching words increases their emotional expressiveness, whereas in bad verse it does not. Of course the versification of a good poem is never continuously regular. Accents are dropped or displaced; unstressed syllables are left out, or extra syllables inserted. But we are, or should be, always conscious of the underlying pattern, the ideal rhythmical base.

Such metrical irregularities are necessary not merely in order to prevent monotony: for any writer who knows his business they are a powerful instrument for controlling and modifying the emotional values of language. In Milton's line,

Transfix us to the bottom of this gulf,

there are only three stressed syllables. If these words were to occur in a news-

paper article we should probably read
them so rapidly that they would not
sound like a blank verse at all. In
order that they may become a verse, we
must either put artificial stresses upon
to and *of*, and read, " Trans- | fíx us |
tó the | bóttom | óf this | gúlf,"
which, though formally a blank verse, is
not English; or else we must linger
upon certain syllables, and stretch
them out sufficiently to compensate
for the absent stresses: " Trans | fíx
us | to the | bóttom | of this | gúlf."
What happens here is something of the
same nature as syncopation in music.
The two pairs of syllables, *-fix us* and
bottom, are each dwelt upon and
prolonged, so that they expand and
bulge over from their own bars into the
bars that follow them, and so push
away the unemphatic syllables *to* and
of from the positions at the beginning
of the bar, where a stress would
normally occur. We are in fact compelled, if the line is to make metrical

sense, to read the words slowly and spaciously, which produces the rhetorical and emotional effect that Milton intended. The following lines from Milton are instances of the opposite process of forcing into the rhythmical mould words which in ordinary prose speech would claim more elbow-room than the metre allows them:

O'er many a frozen, many a fiery alp,
Rocks, caves, lakes, fens, bogs, dens, and shades of death.

The natural way of spacing these words, if they were prose, would be: "Rócks, | cáves, | lákes, | féns, | bógs, | déns, and | shádes of | déath." But the metrical framework compels us to crowd these monosyllables together, and read them twice as rapidly as we should in prose. This hurry and constipation produces an effect of effort and strain, which is just what is required. An extreme case of

this power of metre to mould and so
give life to a phrase, is the line,

And made him bow to the gods of his wives,

If this be read as a line with four
stresses, thus: "And | máde him |
bów to the | góds of his | wíves," it
is then not a Miltonic blank verse at all.
Yet, since we cannot read it, "And |
máde him | bów tó | thé góds | óf
his | wíves," the only thing to be done
is to put a kind of level staccato accent
on the last six syllables, thus: "And
máde him bów tó thé góds óf hís
wíves," which spaces the words out, so
that they sound like a blank verse, or
at least do the best they can to sound
like one. Thus not only is our ear
sufficiently reminded of the underlying
metrical base, but we are obliged to
give to the phrase a kind of fierce
indignant or ironic emphasis, which
again is, I think, exactly what Milton
intended. I could multiply instances;

but these should be sufficient to illustrate the way in which verse, if it be well written, adds imaginative expressiveness to words, by forcing us to space them out and emphasise them, till they acquire new values that they would not have had in prose.

Another obvious function of a constant metrical framework is that of heightening the values of words and phrases by mere position, much as the structure of a cathedral may do with sculpture. Any passage of Milton, or of Keats' mature work, might be used to illustrate this principle.

If then the main function of spoken verse be this of building a framework upon which we may place words in significant and beautiful relations both with each other and with the rhythmical structure itself, and upon which we may also stretch out and contract them, in order to increase their emotional values, it would seem to be necessary that this framework should be definite and constant. And it is this necessity that is, I think, the chief objection to some modern experiments in free verse. Whatever advantages there may be in emancipation from regularity, we should not forget the price that has to be paid for it in the loss or diminution of this power of moulding and vivifying language. It is true that there have been many successful experiments in more or less free verse, from the choruses in *Samson Agonistes* to, let us say, Mr. Waley's translations of early Chinese poetry; but I suggest that as a general rule the success is in proportion to the degree in which we are made aware of a fixed metrical base underlying the irregularities. But what are we to think of this kind of thing?

Come, my songs, let us express our baser passions.
Let us express our envy for the man with a
   steady job and no worry about the future.

Have these words, by being divided

into two lines, acquired any kind of value they would not have had if they had been printed as prose, in which case they might be enjoyed as an amusing satirical outburst? But it would almost seem that at times free verse is no more than an excuse for uttering futilities and ineptitudes that we should not have dared to express in honest prose.

There is yet another important aspect of this medium of modern verse which we must not forget. Ancient poetry was in an obvious and literal sense an incantation, at once charming and exciting the mind through the ear. Now modern poetry, though no longer chanted but spoken, still retains, or should retain, something of its primitive nature as an incantation. It is notorious that poets, when reading verse, generally fall into a kind of chanting delivery, which sometimes, owing to their lack of skill, may seem affected, and even absurd. But their

instinct is none the less right. Poetry
read to sound like prose is intolerable.
Thought is not poetic unless it be
kindled into emotion; and the natural
language of emotion is different from
that of prose, the vehicle of reason.
Not only is it more rhythmical, but it
is more musical; that is to say, though
the pitch is not deliberately regulated,
as in song, there is a tendency to a level
monotonous intonation, and changes of
pitch, when they occur, are more
conscious and more noticeable. The
commonest fault of bad speakers of
verse on the stage is to emphasise
individual words by raising the pitch,
so destroying the music that is proper
to verse, and incidentally the rhythm
too.

And here I may mention a danger to
which both writers and readers of
modern verse are very liable. In order
to get the full value out of poetry (or
indeed out of prose too), we ought,
as Flaubert insisted, to read it aloud.

But as we cannot always be doing that, we must, when reading silently to ourselves, listen with our unsensual ear to the same sounds and the same rhythms, moving at the same pace, as though we were reading aloud. Otherwise we shall not be reading poetry. It is indeed quite possible that twenty lines of Milton, read silently thus, may actually take up somewhat less time than they would if they were read aloud; but the pace ought not to *seem* hurried: in so far as it does, the magic of the medium will be impaired or destroyed. Moreover poets themselves, when, as they often do, they write more for the eye and for the mind than for the ear, are not writing literature at all, let alone poetry.

CHAPTER III

The Evolution of Technique

I HAVE now made it as clear as I am able what I believe the medium of modern spoken verse to be; and I have tried to indicate some of the dangers that lie in wait both for poets and their readers. The best safeguard is that we should fully realise both what the medium is and what it is not. All art consists in exploiting the possibilities and limitations of a medium; and any art of which the medium is misunderstood, and so misused, is likely to degenerate into gracelessness or triviality, and perish as it deserves.

Now that poetry is generally no longer performed, but read, it is obvious that its nature has to a certain extent grown more like that of prose, and that there has been a corresponding increase both in subtlety of expression, and in the possible range of material. Let us take full advantage of this change: but let us also remember that "everything is what it is, and not another thing"; that poetry still is, and always must be, a different art from prose; and that so long as it retains its integrity, it will have its own proper subject-matter, which though it may sometimes resemble, will never be the same as that of any other art.

Let us also honestly admit the truth that poetry has ceased to be a great popular and social art. It is no longer possible for it to be publicly recited or performed in any way. When it ventures upon the stage, it becomes a cause either of boredom or of laughter, unless it be travestied until it is unrecognisable. When associated with music, it is absorbed in the more dominating medium. It is of course possible, though unlikely, that music will evolve in the direction of greater simplicity; or that some few musicians may grow sufficiently interested in poetry to devise a special kind of music, so tenuous and transparent that poetry will be able to live and breathe through it. It is also conceivable that, although the public of the commercial theatre will not tolerate poetry on the stage, satisfactory amateur productions of verse plays may become more common. I have never heard verse spoken on the stage more beautifully than by Ulysses and Agamemnon in the Cambridge Marlowe Society's *Troilus*. If such successes were to become more frequent, we might hope in time to establish a tradition for performing verse plays, and to create a fit audience for them, which would encourage poets to take poetical drama seriously. But if that is to happen, then modern experiments will have to be risked, and produced as carefully and as frequently as classical revivals are now.

But though in this direction we may see a kind of dawning hope for poetical drama, yet I fear it is no more than a dubious glimmering. Poetry will still have to be written in the main for readers. And if poets are to continue to find readers, in spite of the growing competition of the more popular arts of music, the prose drama, the cinema, and the novel, they will have, I fancy, to take thought how they may put away childish things, and become, not perhaps more serious, but more rational, more daring, in fact more interesting. The material for poetry is the whole realm of the sensuous and intellectual imagination, and that is infinite. At present poets seem to be somewhat timid and unenterprising explorers. And I would suggest that experiments and innovations in technique are likely to be the most hopeful means of extending the range of expression and of discovering new material. In every art changes and developments of the medium require and call forth the invention of appropriate subject matter; and the greatest art has always been produced where inspiration has been refreshed and quickened by technical changes, which have made possible the exploitation of unfamiliar themes. It would be rash to foretell with any confidence the directions in which poetical technique will develop in the future. The poets themselves will go their own ways, for better or for worse. But I may perhaps venture to indicate what seeem to me the most natural and profitable lines of development.

Whatever may be our theory as to the true æsthetic and emotional function of metre, the conscious governing principle, according to which English verse has been written from the time of Chaucer until recent years, has been that of syllable-counting. Wherever a decasyllabic line contained more than ten syllables, elision, or the fiction of elision, was assumed as the explanation. Milton indeed formulated for himself certain definite rules, which he observed with great strictness, at least in *Paradise Lost*. But already in Shakespeare we may perceive a tendency to determine rhythm by stress rather than by the number of syllables; and during the last hundred years we find stress becoming more and more the dominant principle of English prosody. When Mr. Abercrombie writes:

> And I will show
> This mask the devil wears, this old shipman,
> A thing to make his proud heart of evil
> Writhe like a trodden snake;

or when Mr. Bottomley writes:

> Have I broken the bird's wings to catch the bird?
> Have I shattered the door of her mind to enter
> there?

they are following the same principle that allowed Shakespeare to say:

> Dearly my delicate Ariel. Let us approach . . .

or again:

Is goads, thorns, nettles, tails of wasps.

They have in fact adopted an entirely different metrical system not only from Milton's, but from such poets as Donne, who when he wrote:

Blasted with sighs, and surrounded with tears,

did so in the confidence that his readers would be instinctively conscious of the number of the syllables, and so would not be disconcerted by the irregular disposition of the stresses.

These two systems of syllabic and stress prosody, though descended from the same parent, the rhymed couplet of Chaucer, have now grown to be very different from each other. I would suggest that, just as stress prosody had its origin in Shakespeare's need for increased energy and emphasis in verse that was intended to be declaimed on the stage, so it may still be found to be the more expressive instrument for dramatic poetry, or for lyrics that require a free rhythmical structure; whereas syllabic prosody, of which Milton was the supreme master, is more suitable for undramatic verse of a deliberate and even movement, or for meditative lyrical poetry, like that of Donne and Keats. In a recently published poem, written in alexandrines, Mr. Bridges has carried the syllabic principle to its logical conclusion, and relying upon the rigid observance of his rule of twelve syllables to each line, has ventured upon a far more extensive use of difficult displacements of accent than even Milton thought possible. It may be that, as often happens with experimental artists, Mr. Bridges has demanded more effort from some of his readers than they will be able to give. But if so, it is to be hoped that he will write more poetry on the same method, so that the counting of syllables may become as natural and instinctive a process with us as it evidently is with him. He has already had the courage to explore the possibilities of English quantitative verse; yet though some of the poetry he wrote according to that system was of remarkable beauty, the experiment was perhaps too alien to the rhythmical genius of our language to be altogether satisfactory. But his new syllabic experiment, being no mere leap in the dark, but a natural development of the medium we have inherited from Chaucer and Milton, deserves our welcome, and is all the more likely to achieve lasting success.

In discussing the structure of English metre, I have taken my examples from blank verse, because that is the oldest and most highly elaborated of our verse-forms. But besides blank verse there are three other fundamental rhythms, each with a history and future possibilities of its own. If a musical analogy be permissible, rhythms of the blank verse kind (with or without rime, and whatever may be the number of feet to the line) may be said to be in duple time. But there is another rhythmical variety, which is sometimes not easy to distinguish from duple time, yet is essentially different.

> And mony was the feather bed
> That flatter'd on the faem;
> And mony was the gude lord's son
> That never mair came hame.

This seven-stressed couplet, in which so many of our ballads are written, may be said to be in common time. The first, third, fifth and seventh stresses are generally stronger than the three intervening stresses, thus producing a kind of rhythmical undulation, which gives the line swiftness and lightness. The Elizabethans used this metre frequently in the form of rimed couplets. Chapman's translation of the *Iliad,* for example, is written in it. Blake in his prophetic books was the first, so far as I know, to dispense with

rime, and to give the line variety by
frequently changing the position of the
cæsura, which normally follows the
fourth stress. The following lines are
from the *Book of Thel.*

The daughters of the Seraphim led round their
    sunny flocks—
All but the youngest: she in paleness sought the
    secret air,
To fade away like morning beauty from her
    mortal day.
Down by the river of Adona her soft voice is
    heard,
And thus her gentle lamentation falls like
    morning dew :—
" O life of this our spring! why fades the lotus
    of the water?
Why fade these children of the spring, born but
    to smile and fall?
Ah! Thel is like a watery bow, and like a part-
    ing cloud;
Like a reflection in a glass; like shadows in the
    water;
Like dreams of infants, like a smile upon an
    infant's face;
Like the dove's voice; like transient day; like
    music in the air."

Shelley uses this metre lyrically in two
of his most beautiful poems, taking the
liberty of omitting the minor even

stresses, and the light syllables that precede them, whenever it suits his purpose.

Awáy! The móor is dárk beneath the moón.
Rápid clouds have drúnk the lást pale beams of éven:
Awáy! the gathering wínds will cáll the darkness sóon,
And profóundest midnight shróud the seréne lights of héaven.

He concludes with the completely filled-out structure:

Thy remémbrance, and repéntance, and deep músings are not frée
From the músic of two vóices and the light of one sweet smíle.

The lines in his *Prometheus* beginning:

Ah Síster, Desolátion is a délicate thíng,

are also written in this metre, which moreover is sufficiently Protean to form the basis of several of Gilbert's most attractive songs, such as, "If

[40]

you're anxious for to shine in the high
æsthetic line as a man of culture rare."
There is no reason why this metre
should not be developed into a very
expressive and subtle instrument,
especially if Blake's experiment be
taken as a starting point. Though it
may not have the grandeur of Milton's
blank verse, it has more rapidity and
lightness, and is not without a beauty
and dignity of its own.

Triple time was seldom employed by
the Elizabethans, except in lyrics such
as Shakespeare's :

Merrily, merrily shall I live now
Under the blossom that hangs on the bough.

The eighteenth century found it an
effective comedic rhythm, as in Gold-
smith's :

When they talked of their Raphaels, Correggios
    and stuff,
He shifted his trumpet and only took snuff.

But it was Shelley who first successfully

slowed down triple time, and gave it dignity and variety, as in his *Sensitive Plant:*

And the jessamine faint, and the sweet tuberose,
The sweetest flower for scent that blows;
And all rare blossoms from every clime
Grew in that garden in perfect prime.

This rhythm has now become, in various forms and disguises, one of our commonest lyrical metres, easily modulating into duple time, and adaptable to lines of various lengths.

There is also another slower triple time, quite different to the usual form. Byron used it, probably without knowing what he was doing, in several of his lyrics, such as the Song of the Third Spirit in *Manfred,* and "There be none of Beauty's daughters": but the only instance I know where it has been consciously and deliberately used, is Professor Murray's translation of an *Ionic a minore* ode in the *Hippolytus:*

Could I take me to some cavern for mine hiding,
In the hill-tops where the Sun scarce hath trod.

[42]

EVOLUTION OF TECHNIQUE

It is unlikely that this difficult rhythm will ever become common; but in lyric poetry, by way of occasional contrast, very beautiful effects might well be obtained by it.

So far as I can see, these four are the only fundamental rhythms in English poetry. Their true nature, their various disguises, and their difference and relationship with one another, are not always sufficiently understood, and the result has frequently been confused and clumsy workmanship, and a failure to exploit their latent possibilities to the full.

There is one further aspect of the poetic craft which I must now mention. The Greek lyrical poets, whose metre was quantitative, and was emphasised by music and dancing movements, were able to build up far more elaborately organised rhythmical structures than we are accustomed to, with our simpler lyrical forms. Structure, with us, is generally delineated and emphasised by

rime, rather than by internal varia-
tions and contrasts of rhythm. Even
in the unrimed choruses of *Samson
Agonistes* the rhythm is far more
uniform than in the simplest Greek
lyrical poems. I do not suggest that
it would be possible or desirable
artificially to change the nature of
English poetical rhythm from an accen-
tual to a quantitative basis, as
Ennius did with Latin prosody. But
although no doubt purely quantitative
English verse will always remain somewhat of an exotic curiosity, I feel sure
that if more conscious attention were
paid to the quantity of English syllables,
not only would our normal verse-forms,
such as blank verse, gain in subtlety
and expressive force, but all sorts of
new possibilities of lyrical structure
could be discovered and explored. Rime
need not necessarily be dispensed with;
but it would no longer be the only effective instrument for binding together
a complicated lyrical stanza. Stress

would still indicate and govern internal rhythm; but careful attention to the length and shortness of syllables would make it possible to build up far more elaborate and varied metrical structures than have hitherto been attempted. The result might be a verse that was genuinely free, yet did not degenerate into prose, based upon irregular but easily comprehensible metrical patterns, that could mould and dominate language as effectively as the older, more rigid verse-forms.

CHAPTER IV

Poetic Material

DIFFICULT as it must be to foresee the evolution of technical methods, it would be still more hazardous to attempt any prediction as to the new subject-matter which poets will have to discover, if their art is to continue as a living growth. The mind of even the most detached artist is a part of the world into which he was born, and his matter must to a large extent be a reflection of his environment. But the material and spiritual world changes far more swiftly than the language and the rhythmical artifices which constitute the poetic medium. And so, although I have suggested elsewhere that technique is the mistress of invention,

[47]

and that changes in the medium make possible the discovery of new themes, yet an opposite theory might as easily be maintained, with perhaps equal truth, that social and intellectual changes create demands, in satisfying which an intelligent artist will find his most genial inspiration, and will modify his technique until it becomes a fit instrument for expressing his new material. But though for these reasons it would be unwise to indulge in prophecy, we may at least take a survey of the main possibilities.

To begin with, the innumerable and infinite output of personal lyrics, good, bad and indifferent, is certain to continue, so long as human beings are subject to passions and sentimentalities, and can enjoy the varying moods of nature, and the pleasures of poetic pastiche. However capriciously the winds of literary fashion may blow, the countless flock of minor lyricists will always be with us, while the truly great will be few and far between. One danger indeed we have little reason to fear. I mean the sterilising tyranny of some dominant lyrical form, such as the Greek elegiac couplet, or the late-classical Chinese stanza. Our poetry is already so abundantly rich in types, and so fertile in breeding new varieties, that neither the spirit of a new Age, nor genius however individual need be at a loss for appropriate forms of lyrical self-expression. A twentieth-century Catullus or Heine would have no cause for complaint if he were to be born an Englishman.

It is with regard to lyrics on a larger, more elaborate scale, that English poets have hitherto shown least ambition and enterprise. The Pindarics of Gray are a poor substitute for Pindar; while the *Odes* of Keats and Matthew Arnold's *Thyrsis* and *Scholar-Gipsy* are elegiac rather than lyrical in mood and form. Shelley and Goethe, and at times Swinburne, have shown them-

selves to be more truly the successors
of the greater Greek lyric poets; and
if they be rightly understood, their
example may yet bear fruit for our
delight of altogether unimaginable
quality. But the tendency of the
moment seems to be towards poems on
a small scale, of a somewhat anæmic
delicacy, or else of an artful and piquant
quaintness, rather than towards the
sustained movement, and elaborate
yet highly organised form, which is
necessary for the greatest lyrical poetry.

Another province of literature, which
we have seldom as yet attempted to
make our own, is that of comic poetry.
We have indeed had many and various
comic writers of first-rate quality; but
although, when they were so minded,
Chaucer and Shakespeare and Byron
could show themselves to be masters
of comedy in verse, we have as yet
had no Aristophanes, but have been
obliged to content ourselves with the
charming trivialities and vulgarities of

a Gilbert. If only Ben Jonson, in
addition to stage-craft, Gargantuan
comic energy and Titanic eloquence,
had been gifted with a particle of that
fiery celestial ether, by which alone
mortal art can become divine, then
indeed perhaps . . . But of what
use are regrets? The future, not the
past, is here our concern. And what a
future might there not be for the comic
genius who should be so fortunately
inspired as to take the popular Farce,
or even the theatrical Revue, and by
giving it the life and the wings of
poetry, so transform it from a poor
ephemeral stage-hobby-horse into an im-
mortal cloud-cruising Pegasus, or at
least a serviceable Hippogryph! Thus
sublimely mounted, what regions of the
earth and sky might not such a Beller-
ophon explore? What monsters and
Chimæras might he not torment and
slay with the shafts of his lyrical
ridicule? All that men and women
say or think or do, would lie ready as

fuel for his imagination to kindle at
will, all our follies and fashions, vices
and virtues, stupidities, cruelties, noble
extravagances, religious and metaphysical dreams. If Socrates could
afford to be a good-naturedly amused
spectator of the *Clouds,* so might Freud
of some *Comedy of Dreams* by our
modern Aristophanes: and if he could
not, why, so much the worse for him
and his speculations. How wholesome
too for our prominent statesmen and
demagogues!—But alas, I am forget-
ting our Lord Chamberlain. We are
not yet sufficiently enlightened to tolerate political caricature and Rabelaisian
ribaldry upon our stage, and an English
Knights or *Lysistrata* must remain, I
fear, for the present a poet's dream.
Nevertheless, under a reasonably
intelligent censorship, what Rabelais
was for his age, an emancipated
imaginative comedy might well be for
our own, except that, whereas the
Gallic genius has always expressed itself

most naturally and completely in prose, ours would expand more congenially into poetry, which, for all its apparent limitations, should be, at its best, the more universal interpreter of the spirit of man, whether on the plane of tragedy or of comedy.

There is good reason for hoping that the problem of an adequate stage-performance of imaginative comedy would be less difficult to solve than it seems to be in the case of serious poetic drama. Actors are always more ready to understand and do justice to plays that are good fun as well as good literature. Mr. Bernard Shaw and Gilbert and Sullivan are apt to meet with better treatment at the hands of our producers and performers than Ibsen or Wagner. All the same even poetic tragedy should not be too lightly despaired of. If great plays can be written, someone sooner or later is likely to have the ambition and the intelligence to produce them worthily. Something of the kind

seems to have happened at Glasgow, in
the case of Mr. Gordon Bottomley's
verse plays. Let us hope, however
cautiously, that what Scotland does
to-day, England may at least begin to
think of doing to-morrow. Meantime
there is one wholesome lesson that poets
may learn from the undoubted literary
success of Mr. Bottomley's *Gruach* and
Lear's Wife. It is continually being
dinned into their ears by critics who
should know better, that the time is
now gone by when poets might borrow
their material from a remote or legendary past; that a twentieth-century
dramatist must deal only in twentieth-
century themes if he hopes to reach the
hearts of twentieth-century men and
women, or to win the good graces of
Georgian reviewers. And yet it is
unquestionably true that in every
period when poetic tragedy has flour-
ished, mythical, legendary and historical
subjects have been the rule, and contemporary themes the rare exceptions.

Oedipus, Agamemnon and Pentheus
were not fifth-century Athenians any
more than Hamlet, Lear and Antony
were Elizabethans, or Andromaque and
Phèdre *Parisiennes* of the *grand siècle*.
The artistic success of the *Persae*,
Othello and *Bajazet* merely make this
determined preference for archaic
subject-matter seem the more remarkable. And yet none of these writers
were mere literary antiquarians, but
true children of their own age, to whose
dramas we now look first, if we wish to
understand the mentality and the
moral standards of the populace that
applauded them. Even Goethe, in the
work that perhaps more than any other
represents the complexity of modern
ideas and aspirations, went back to a
myth that was then two hundred years
old. It would seem as though the
poetic imagination, when it sets itself
the most arduous of its tasks, that of
alembicating tragic beauty from human
misery and passion, welcomes the limi-

tation of choice, the simplicity of atmosphere, the freedom from distracting contemporary preoccupations, which a remote theme brings with it. None the less Ibsen's *Brandt* and *Peer Gynt* show how a modern, though scarcely a familiar world, may be made the background of true poetic tragedy; although in *Peer Gynt* the almost continued presence of the Comedic Muse, with her incurable modernity, tempers the difficulty of the problem. Thus, though it would be unreasonable to maintain that the Tragic Muse must be unable to live and breathe in the smoky atmosphere of our present-day world, it would be still more absurd to prohibit her escape into the purer clime of a legendary or historical past.

The case of narrative poetry is somewhat similar, yet with important differences. It is true that the Homeric heroes and the society in which they lived had long ceased to exist when the *Iliad* and the *Odyssey* were composed, and that most of the great epic and narrative writers, Virgil, Ariosto, Milton and Marlowe, preferred mythical or purely fantastic settings for their stories. Yet such a limitation would seem to be hardly so natural to narrative as to tragic poetry. For the quality of narrative being less intense and passionate, and its unity more loose, it is able to indulge copiously in decoration, description and digression, and so should be able to deal all the more effectively with the variegated modern scene. And yet, except for two sombre short stories in blank verse by Wordsworth, and Byron's *Don Juan*, there has scarcely been any narrative, dealing with modern life and of first-rate poetical quality, since Chaucer's *Canterbury Tales*. This is perhaps because poets have not sufficiently realised that the telling of a story in verse instead of prose can only be justified when the sensuous and decorative beauty of the medium is continually maintained at the highest pitch. For whereas in the intense and tragic moments of drama exquisiteness and richness of texture may be unnecessary, or at times even a positive nuisance, bald and graceless verse narrative is always insupportable. Byron indeed atoned for much artistic unscrupulousness and slovenly workmanship by his unfailing energy and wit. But poets will have to take to heart the lesson of Chaucer's scrupulous attention to beauty of texture, if they are to hold their own in rivalry with prose fiction. They will have also to be aware of the dangers of a too exclusive interest in analytical psychology. Narrative, when it ceases to narrate, very easily becomes a bore. Such writers as Proust and Henry James may have been able successfully to dispense with many of the functions of story-telling, by laboriously evolving a peculiar prose instrument of their own for the expression of psychological subtleties. But it is doubtful whether anything of the kind would be possible in verse, or, if possible, whether it would be readable. Yet for the direct presentation, serious or humoristic, of character, mood and emotion, verse in the hands of a master will always remain an instrument of supreme power.

There are certain other kinds of poetry, more or less akin to narrative, for which an interesting future may be predicted. The Victorians seem to have had a special predilection for the Dramatic Monologue, perhaps because they unconsciously felt their inability to cope with the problems of drama. *Caliban upon Setebos* and *The Bishop orders his Tomb in St. Praxed's Church* are notable successes; but several of Browning's experiments should be a warning of the danger of lengthiness and over-elaboration in a form that allows of very little narrative interest or dramatic contrast. Great and sustained beauty of language can alone justify a long poem of such a kind; and it is just in this respect that Browning was most deficient.

Another attractive sub-species of narrative poetry is the Dramatic Dialogue or Interlude, which has lately been successfully revived by Mr. Sturge Moore and Mr. Abercrombie. The great master of this form, as also of the Monologue, is Theocritus, whose *Syracusan Women, Kyniska, Thyrsis,* and *Simaitha* will always remain as a challenging inspiration to succeeding ages. The great range of his material within the narrow limits of his surviving work, and his marvellous blend of naturalism and poetry, should be peculiarly suggestive to a generation like our own, with its eagerness to find new paths, or rediscover old ones, to poetic freedom.

It would be presumptuous in one who is not himself a philosopher to speak with assurance about philosophic poetry: yet I shall venture upon some

obvious reflections. Few would dispute
that there has been only one specifically
philosophical work which is also a great
poem, the *De Rerum Natura* of Lucretius. But those of us who love it best
will, if we are candid, admit that it
contains vast tracts of scientific and
metaphysical discussion, which even
fervid and eloquent genius has not
wholly succeeded in clothing with the
vesture of poetry. It is true that, for
those few who have the courage and
wisdom to read them, these sections
should have a very high value as parts
of a sublime imaginative vision of the
universe; and they also contain many
scattered episodes of divine poetic
loveliness. But the claim of Lucretius
to rank among the world's greatest
writers will always rest upon those
sections, such as the endings of his
third, fourth and fifth books, where the
material is already in its essence poetic,
and gives scope to his supreme gift for
sensuous description, or for passionate

ethical discourse. It is to be feared
that if a poet of equal genius with
Lucretius were to take modern psychology, the physics of Einstein, or the
philosophy of Mr. Russell as his subject-
matter, with the intention of seriously
expounding and not of merely poetising
them, he would be unable to avoid
similar desert tracts of unpoetical
reasoning. But it is a narrow view
which can deny that verse should ever
be employed, unless the result be
poetry. If an artist in language is
able to set forth philosophic matter
that is of great intrinsic interest more
luminously and attractively in verse
than could be done in prose (which is
precisely what Lucretius did with the
crabbed sentences of Epicurus), let us
not grudge him the praise and gratitude
that are his due. However, it seems
unlikely that scientific philosophy will
ever again inspire an expository
treatise such as the *De Rerum Natura*.
It might indeed enter as an all-pervad-

ing influence into some comprehensive epic design, just as religion and scholastic philosophy pervade the *Divina Commedia*. What is certain is that, as there have always been, so there always will be philosophically minded poets, and that they will discover for themselves what forms serve their purpose best.

The treatise, as a poetic form, would seem to be more suitable for subjects that are neither strictly philosophic, nor scientific. Yet though we have had our *Seasons, Night Thoughts,* and *Sofas* in plenty, Virgil's *Georgics* remain still unrivalled. Why should not an ingenious and erudite poet take some such pregnant subject as Architecture, the Garden, or the Evolution of Religion, or if he have the knowledge and the boldness, Machinery, Medicine or Economics, and dispute Virgil's supremacy in this field, as Virgil once did Hesiod's? How fascinating would he not find the problem of wedding

didactic and historical exposition to
perfect loveliness of texture? What
opportunities for description and
reflection? And with what entrancing
episodes, serious or playful, might he
not delight our fancy?

Not the least noble, nor the least
exacting of mistresses, is the Muse of
Satire. *"Facit indignatio versum,"*
said Juvenal. But alas, how fumbling
a designer, how banal a metrician, how
unscrupulous and inartistic a poetaster
has Indignation generally proved her-
self to be. Few satires survive the
ephemeral social follies that provoked
them, because, being by nature parasites,
when that which supported their growth
decays and perishes, they too must
perish, unless indeed they are rooted
deeply in the unchanging soil of imagination and poetry. Truly great satire
will always be very rare. It is still
possible to read with delight Byron's
Vision of Judgment, and portions of his
Age of Bronze; and there are passages

in Pope and Dryden that fully deserve
their reputation. But it is perhaps only
in parts of the *Divina Commedia,* and
in the last three hundred lines of the
fourth book of Lucretius, and occasionally in Leopardi, that satire may be
found mingled as the dominating
element in poetry of the highest order.
Its taste even there is bitter, but with
the divine bitterness of passion and
sincerity.

In the enchanted kindom of fantasy
and the mock-heroic, Pope's *Rape of
the Lock* and Lear's poems still reign
supreme. It is perhaps because they
are ostensibly written for the delight
of children, that *The Owl and the
Pussycat, The Dong,* and the *Quangle-
Wangle* have never, so far as I know,
found their way into serious adult an-
thologies. Yet if we are really sincere
in our quest for lyrical beauty, verbal
euphony and metrical invention, we
should not have tolerated without pro-
test the absence of these poems from the

Oxford Book of Verse, where they would more than hold their own in the company of *Annabel Lee, The Lady of Shalott,* and *The Blessed Damozel.*

CHAPTER V

MISCELLANEOUS

THE main trouble with all attempts at
literary classification is that they are
bound to exclude many intermediate
types. Much of the most memorable
English poetry is neither in a strict
sense lyrical, nor philosophic, nor anything else than beautiful and shapely
verse. No other literature is so rich
as ours in quasi-lyrical poetry, such as
the sonnets of Shakespeare and Wordsworth, Gray's *Elegy* and Keats' *Odes*.
Future writers will doubtless invent
other similar forms for their new purposes; but it would be a disastrous
error to suppose that, because an art-
form has once become classical, it
therefore can no longer be used, except

for academic pastiche. No form is ever
superannuated if it be the best possible
vehicle for expressing a new artistic
idea. A poet need be no more afraid
of using the Shakespearian or Petrarch-
ian sonnet, than a musician need be
ashamed of composing a classical fugue,
provided his inspiration be genuine;
and its genuineness will not be obscured
or destroyed by being cast into some old
and well-tried mould. Indeed the most
truly academic works are often those
in which some ephemerally fashionable
formula has been blindly adopted
without being understood. The
mental habits of poets are as various
as those of scientists or politicians.
Wordsworth, who far more than most
poets drew his material from his own
experience, was nevertheless inspired
to invent his most felicitous work by
such traditional forms as the sonnet or
the common ballad stanza: his *Ode
to Duty* is exactly modelled on a metrical invention of Gray, and the pattern

of his *Leech-Gatherer*, but for one slight variation, is the same as that of Shakespeare's *Rape of Lucrece*. On the other hand Walt Whitman spent many years laboriously floundering in search of a poetic method, and it was only late in life that his unconscious sense of form led him to write a few poems that are as perfect in design and as moving as any fragment of Alcman.

In every fertile and creative age of literature, it will generally be found that there were two main stimulating influences at work: in the first place naturalism, or an awakened sensitiveness to the suggestive beauty of the actual world; and secondly the fascination exercised by the masterpieces of earlier periods and alien cultures. By this I do not mean the direct inheritance of a poetic medium. Milton no doubt learnt his metrical technique from Shakespeare and the Elizabethans, but in everything else he owed far more to his loving study of Homer, Euripides,

Virgil and the Bible. Thus too the spiritual presence of Homer is felt everywhere in the Greek lyrical and dramatic writers, and even in Theocritus; and thus emulous idolatry of Greek and Alexandrine masterpieces quickened into life all that was best in Latin poetry; while Virgil and Ovid in their turn became the schoolmasters of Dante and the Renaissance. The tyranny of Latin over English poetry only began to wane towards the end of the eighteenth century; then suddenly in Shelley and Keats, and later in Matthew Arnold, Swinburne, Mr. Bridges, and even Browning, the Hellenic spirit becomes a veritable Castalian fountain of inspiration. Now that the knowledge of Greek is likely to become a rare accomplishment, it is possible that its influence will die away as quickly as it flowered. Yet the imagination is sometimes kindled by translations even more potently than by scholarship, as is shown by the case

of Keats, who had small Latin and less
Greek. And indeed, apart from our
ever-growing interest in our own earlier
literature, the most helpful and fertile
impulse seems likely in the near future
to come through translations of Oriental poetry, such as those by Mr. Waley
and Mr. Nicholson. But from whatever direction the wind may blow, it
will be the most imaginative artists who
will first be sensitive to it, and the
most skilful and discreet in the use they
put it to. The lesser crowd will, as
ever, follow their lead, until what was
once a renovating breath of inspiration
has become a stale and flatulent
academicism.

Even if it be true, as I have suggested
earlier in this essay, that poetry has
ceased to be a great popular and social
art, there will be no need to regret the
change in so far as it may make it more
easy for poets to disregard fashionable
success, and so to retain their artistic
integrity. Yet there are certain

dangers to which they will become
increasingly liable. An art which pre-
supposes a select initiated audience,
very quickly becomes over-precious,
and, for all its refinement, essentially
parochial. The best art will take
nothing for granted in those to whom it
is addressed, except artistic intelligence
and that human nature which is common to us all. Poets whose idiom is not
universal, but calculated for a cultured
private coterie, write with the risk of
swift oblivion, so soon as the tide of
æsthetic caprice has turned. This is
all the more regrettable, as such poetry
is sometimes of great originality and
beauty. The most frequent fault is
obscurity, due either to an Alexandrine
love of recondite allusions, or more
often to an apparently studied neglect
of transitions. A contempt for clarity
has almost come to be regarded as an
artistic virtue, rather than as a vice, or
at best an occasionally inevitable evil.
Nothing in truth can be more funda-

mentally inartistic than needless obscurity. Poetry that is intellectually and emotionally complex, is certain in any case to be difficult enough; and the less a reader is called upon to make avoidable mental effort, the more convincingly will the essential context of a poem be communicated to his mind. The medium of poetry consists not merely of words, but of speech, that is of words, phrases and sentences in syntactic and logical relations to one another; and although these relations necessarily tend to be more emotional and less rational in poetry than in prose, because poetry is the more emotional medium, yet there are limits which it is dangerous to exceed. Much no doubt depends upon the nature of the subject matter. A chorus of Aeschylus, or a soliloquy of Macbeth may be very difficult to analyse and construe satisfactorily; yet their general drift is usually clear enough. Cloudy vagueness or intricate subtlety may well be necessary and legitimate qualities of a poem; but all superfluous obscurity is æsthetically pure waste. Gerard Hopkins is a deplorable example of a poet of sincerity and genius, who damaged much of his best work by not being sufficiently aware of the nature of his instrument, which was the English language, or of his audience, who could only be educated English-speaking people. The admirers of such writers will often quite honestly deny that they find them unduly difficult. They probably forget how hard they have had to work in order to obtain their reward. The trouble is that the poet ought to have done the larger part of their work for them himself.

Whatever may be the destinies of English poetry, I do not think it is likely to achieve anything very remarkable until we have grown out of a doctrine or prejudice that is widely prevalent just now, that is to say our dislike and suspicion of rhetoric. By rhetoric I mean the sum of all the artifices and habits of syntax, phrasing and diction which are necessary in order to sustain the movement and the structure of a poem that is designed on a large scale, or of a short poem of great emotional intensity. That may be a loose and unsatisfactory definition, but it is the best I can come by. Criticism nowadays seems to be mainly interested in lyrical poetry on a small scale; and this may account for the disfavour into which the very name of rhetoric has fallen: for it is true that short lyrics of a certain kind can afford to dispense with rhetoric, in the sense in which I am using the word. Yet if the European poets of the past, and their public, had been as shy of rhetoric as we are at present, it is certain that there would have been no Homer to begin with, still less an Aeschylus, a Milton, a Racine, or a Shelley. We might have produced poetry of exquisite charm and refinement, but its imagina-

tive range and vitality would probably
have been as restricted as that of the
Japanese, or of the later Chinese poets.
If we compare in Mr. Waley's translations the classical Tang poets with those
earlier primitive writers, who were
not yet afraid of composing on a fairly
large scale, we shall then see what may
be the fate of a literature that has
grown ashamed of employing the
breadth and energy of movement without which great poetry is impossible.
Of course there has always been, and
always will be, bad rhetoric, as well as
good. The inferior imitators of Milton,
for instance, used to impose upon their
own commonplace poetic conceptions
the whole stylistic apparatus which
Milton had elaborated for the purpose
of sustaining the enormous movement
of his verse, and enriching its texture.
Bad rhetoric is always stale rhetoric.
" No bird," as Blake says, " soars too
high, if he soars with his own wings."

But it is an ill wind that blows nobody any good; and we may gratefully welcome this impatience of rhetoric, in so far as it serves to purify the air of that pestilential blight which is known as " poetic," but would be more truthfully named " prosaic diction." To quote Mr. Santayana, " when use has worn down a poetic phrase to its external import, and rendered it an indifferent symbol for a particular thing, that phrase has become prosaic. It has also become, by the same process, transparent and purely instrumental." Poetry, when it is healthy and vigorous, is continually discarding such worn-out words and phrases, as being indeed no longer poetical enough for its purposes. It is the simpler, homelier words and idioms of everyday speech that carry with them most poetic suggestion. Not but what rare and far-fetched diction may not on fit occasions be ornamentally useful, or justify itself by its grandeur and impressiveness. Shakespeare knew his business when he wrote,

" The multitudinous seas incarnadine ";
but how thankful we should have been
if succeeding poets had had the wisdom
to refrain from debasing his coinage!
Poetry need not be always simple,
sensuous or passionate; but when it
wishes to be decorative or extravagant,
it will do well to remember the fable of
the jay in peacock's feathers, and grow
novel and appropriate plumage of its
own.

With regard to poetic inversion, there
is bound to be great divergence both
in practice and in critical taste. Swinburne considered Ben Jonson's line,
" But might I of Jove's nectar sup,"
to be an inexcusable blemish in an
otherwise perfect masterpiece. Yet
Jacobean readers would probably have
found the order of the words sufficiently
natural and unforced. It is true that
since then there has been a considerable
change in our linguistic sense, due in
part to the long dominance of prose
during the eighteenth century, and in

part to the waning influence of Latin. Nevertheless even now the best writers in their most genuinely poetic moments still assert for themselves, though within narrower limits, the licence of modifying the strict grammatical order. This surely is as it ought to be; for though a language like ours, which has shed most of its inflections, is compelled to have a more rigid word-order than an inflected language like Latin, yet emotional stress and the need for rhetorical emphasis will always, even in prose, tempt writers to violate the conventional rules, and still more in poetry, where the position of words and phrases in relation to the line is of such paramount importance.

CHAPTER VI

The Children of Thamyris

THERE is another legend concerning
the ancient Hellenic Muses, which I
would here like to recall. It is said that
one of their most gifted and distinguished pupils, the Thessalian bard
Thamyris, having made certain innovations in the orthodox technique of
poetry, and having moreover enlarged
its boundaries by annexing subject-
matter that had hitherto been considered
beneath the dignity of classic art, one
day had the audacity to challenge his
august schoolmistresses to a contest of
song. Apollo was the umpire, and he,
as might have been expected, adjudged
the victory to his divine relatives. The
presumptuous mortal was condemned
to lose his eyes, and forbidden hence-

forth to practise the sacred art of poesy. The baser medium of prose would be good enough for such renegade impostors. But the result was far different from what the Goddesses had expected. Thamyris, though blinded, remained recalcitrant, and retaining all his former skill and genius, like his remote descendants, blind Maeonides and Milton, continued to produce masterpiece after masterpiece. Worse still, he became a popular hero among the miserable mortal multitude, who naturally sided with the victim of divine jealousy. Moreover Thamyris soon afterwards became the father of a numerous family, and their descendants, multiplying throughout the world, inherited, not his blindness, but his poetical gifts. Thus it comes about that all true poets and lovers of poetry are children of Thamyris, and little though they know it, have each some few drops of his inspired and rebellious blood running in their veins. If the

Muses had wished effectively to stamp out heresy, they would have been wiser had they followed the example of Apollo, who flayed alive that other æsthetic mutineer, Marsyas, thus robbing him not only of life, but of the hope of heretical offspring.

Now it appears to me that this tale must have been a prophetic fable, intended to symbolise certain important aspects of man's poetic evolution. If the Muses and Apollo represent the established, conservative tradition of poetry, then in Thamyris must be embodied the perennial revolt of the creative younger generation against the prestige and authority of the past. Though the penalty of rebellion may sometimes be blindness, egoism and eccentricity, yet the sacred fire will remain alive in the heart of the rebel, and will be handed down by him to his posterity, who, themselves neither blind nor mutinous, will often become in turn the persecutors of their own children. Thus the divine flame will never cease to burn, and generation after generation the youth of poetry will be renewed.

Nevertheless there are those who take a gloomier view of man's destinies. Poetry, they tell us, like mythology, religion and metaphysics, is a primitive and puerile function of the human mind. It is already becoming superseded by less rudimentary, more rational means of self-expression. We are entering upon an era of science and prose, and may as well at once frankly put away poetry, along with other childish things. At the beginning of this essay I have tried to suggest how much and how little truth there may be in this view. I have admitted that the dissociation of poetry from music and intonation has to a great extent diminished the immediate potency of its sensuous and emotional appeal; but I have argued that the new medium of spoken verse, although it may have grown more similar to prose, is yet very far from being identical with it, either formally, or in the nature of its subject-matter. Prose is the more transparent, self-effacing instrument. Its value consists not so much in itself (though it may possess a real sensuous charm and beauty of its own), but rather in its intellectual content and the knowledge it conveys. But the value of poetry resides primarily in the medium itself. If that be not beautiful, then verse is a thing of naught, and worse than naught. None the less poetry should be no mere meaningless verbal incantation, nor yet a melodious transmitter of congenial lies and irresponsible reverie. It is a means of discourse, of which the content should be neither science nor history nor speculation in their abstract purity, but all these and much else besides, enveloped and humanised by emotion, and presented with all the moving pathos and beauty which is inherent in them, but which the less imaginative prosaic medium cannot so effectually reveal. So long as human nature remains what it is now, as in spite of cynical prognostications it is likely to do for some time to come, it will both demand and obtain satisfaction for its ideal needs from literature, as well as from the musical and plastic arts: and in fact, if verse were to be proscribed or abandoned by general consent, we should be soon compelled to find an awkward substitute for it in rhythmical or poetic prose. Yet, in spite of the beauty and grandeur of our translations of biblical Hebrew verse, and of certain majestical passages in such writers as Sir Thomas Browne, rhythmical prose has seldom proved itself able to compete with formal poetry. It is too primitive, too monotonous and cumbersome to perform more than a small part of the various functions of modern spoken verse, to which we should inevitably be driven before long to revert.

Yet though the disappearance of poetry is unlikely, and would be a real disaster, it is much to be desired that poetry should become more rational and responsible, more intelligently aware of the best interests and ideals of its most civilised contemporaries. It would be childish and unwise for poets to disregard the fact that our habits of mind are growing continually more scientific. The function of the imagination is to interpret and illuminate reality, and it cannot therefore neglect or despise the normal aspects under which reality presents itself to the human mind. But it must also appeal to the human heart; and since the passions and dreams of the heart are less mutable than the intellect, it is in this respect that the nature of poetry is least likely to suffer any fundamental change. The garment in which it clothes itself will alter, as language alters, and as poets of genius are moved to enlarge or contract it. As long as men use articulate speech,

some few among them will take delight
in moulding it into rhythmical forms of
harmonious beauty, in order to find
the most perfect expression for the
intimate desires and movements of
the soul.

Perhaps I should have been more
prudent if I had confined my discussion
to the more purely technical aspect of
poetry, without venturing upon the
dangerous sea of general reflections
upon style and theme, attitude and
tendency. I have at least tried to refrain from dogma and prophecy, and
attempted rather to suggest future possibilities by drawing attention to the
lessons which we can still learn from
the past. It may well be that the only
really profitable discussions about poetry
are technical discussions. " The thought
of man is not triable. Even the Devil
knoweth not the thought of man," said
the old legal maxim. And so, to my
mind, the thought, the soul of the Muse
of modern poetry is not triable, nor

discussable; but her actions are. And what else are her actions but her successes and failures in exploiting her medium? Although her golden age may seem to lie in the past, and her future be uncertain and beset with perils, yet there is no need to despair of her salvation. To revert to the apologue with which I began, though I may feel some sympathy with the celestial point of view, I am not really on the side of the angels.